HEART'S HOME
Lyndon B. Johnson's Hill Country

by Rose Houk

SOUTHWEST PARKS AND MONUMENTS ASSOCIATION
TUCSON, ARIZONA

Gratitude is extended for the hospitality and generous amounts of time and expertise freely given by the staff of the Lyndon B. Johnson National Historical Park. Special thanks goes to Edwin Bearss of the National Park Service for providing a draft of the Johnson Ranch Operation Study, and to Ava Johnson Cox, who shared her memories and feelings on an August afternoon in Johnson City. Finally, to T. J. Priehs and Michael Collier, appreciation for constructive criticism of the manuscript and unflagging support.

—R. H.

Copyright 1986 by Southwest Parks and Monuments Association, Tucson, Arizona
ISBN 0-911408-66-5   Library of Congress Number 85-62799

SECOND EDITION

Produced in conjunction with the National Park Service staff
at Lyndon B. Johnson National Historical Park

Editorial
T.J. Priehs, Carolyn Dodson

Design
Larry Lindahl Design

Production
Sandra Scott, Laura Symms

Maps
Deborah Reade

Photography
Austin Statesman, courtesy Lyndon B. Johnson Library: 14-15.
Mike Geissinger, courtesy Lyndon B. Johnson Library: 27 (bottom).
Johnson Family Photos, courtesy Lyndon B. Johnson Library: title page, 11, 12 (top), 16, 17 (bottom), 18 (top), 19 (bottom), 20, 21 (bottom), 22-23, 26 (top).
Lyndon B. Johnson Library: 8–9, 10, 17 (top), 21 (top), 22 (left), 29 (bottom).
Robert Knudsen, courtesy Lyndon B. Johnson Library: 24-25.
Frank Muto, courtesy Lyndon B. Johnson Library: 26 (bottom).
Y. R. Okamoto, courtesy Lyndon B. Johnson Library: contents page, 28 (top), 29 (top), 30 (top).
Laurence Parent: 4–5, 6, 7, 13, 18 (bottom), 27 (top), 28 (bottom), back cover.
John Oldenkamp & Cynthia Sabransky: 12 (bottom), 19 (top).
Frank Wolfe, courtesy Lyndon B. Johnson Library: cover, 30 (bottom), 31.

♻ Printed on recycled paper

cover: The Johnsons at the ranch, July 1968
back cover: Morning fog blankets the Texas Hill Country
title page: Johnson children (Lyndon standing) outside the boyhood home, 1915
opposite: LBJ and his beagle, 1965

Contents

Introduction	5
Johnson Country	9
The Fledgling Years	15
Heart's Home	25
Bibliography	32

Sauer-Beckman Farm, LBJ State Historical Park, representative of area farms of the early 1900s

Introduction

The voices of grandfathers still ring clear in the Texas Hill Country. A conversation with a resident rarely progresses far before the inevitable phrase, "My grandpa used to say..." introduces a story. These people knew their roots long before it became fashionable to trace one's family history.

Lyndon Johnson was fond of quoting his ancestors. He, too, lived in the Hill Country, like his father and his father's father before him. In a distance of less than a quarter mile, Lyndon Baines Johnson was born and is buried. He remembered his beginnings, and he was drawn back to the hills throughout his life, as he said, "to refill my cup, to recharge myself."

It could be the tenacious stone fences, crumbling now and partly hidden by brush, or the solid hand-hewn limestone barns beside the road, or the cool shade cast by a venerable live oak. All seem artfully designed to make a person want to come back, to remember.

"Elemental" is a word that applies well to the Hill Country. Its essentials are sun, rock, and water. This is the beginning of the Texas "big sky" country, where the grays give way to blues and the horizon opens out like a pair of big arms. A definite line traces the boundary of the Hill Country and helps to explain the hills' existence. That line is the Balcones Escarpment, which swings in an arc across the midriff of Texas from north of Austin southwest to Del Rio.

On the low side of the break the rich blackland prairies ease out to the coastal flats. On the high side rise the limestone hills which from the air create a pattern of huge scalloped paisleys.

But the Devil's Backbone, as some people prefer to call the escarpment, separates far more than geologic provinces. It spells thin variable soils subject to unpredictable and at times altogether too little rainfall. Early settlers who were unaware of this radical change in the character of the land found life in the Hill Country difficult, if not impossible.

The lovely, hardy bluebonnets, as much a trademark of Texas as Stetson hats, can thrive in the caliche-packed soil. Tall grasses, juicy and delectable to grazing animals, also knew the secrets of the hills. But newcomers from the East, having heard overblown promises of wealth and good fortune to be skimmed from the land, did not have time to learn. The demands of food and shelter were imminent. They did not discover soon enough the "new formula" of living that historian Walter Prescott Webb said the Plains demanded.

Texas bluebonnets and Indian paintbrush

So farmers from the South and Midwest and colonists from Germany obtained title to "good land"—land where the soil was a little deeper and the ground flatter. Fruit trees fared well in the sandy valley soils, as did cotton and milo. Cattle were bred and turned loose on oak- and cedar-covered hillsides, until finally the native grasses were eaten to the quick. The cedars lost no time moving in to claim the newly vacated niches that the grasses once occupied.

A careful observer, driving along U.S. Highway 290 west of Austin to Johnson City, might notice a few clumps of spiny

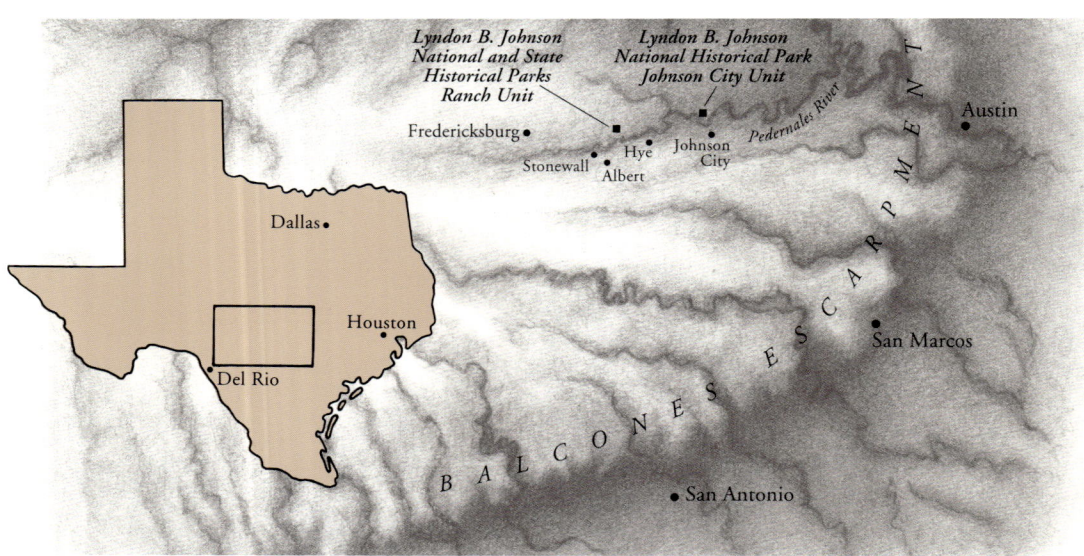

Limestone bluff overlooking Texas Hill Country

Introduction

green flat pads. These prickly pear cactus signal the first tinges of aridity. Perhaps the settlers wondered about these alien plants, but soon they knew. Two years of searing drought could mean an end to a system of livelihood that could not accommodate the vagaries of water supply. The thirty-inch rainfall line slithers sinuously south through the Texas Hill Country like a desert sidewinder, uncomfortably close to the one hundredth meridian, where dryness forced total alteration of agricultural practices.

Many Hill Country pioneers felt the pain of defeat. Some gave up and left for good, like the one who chalked this inscription on his Blanco County log cabin:

250 miles to nearest post office
100 miles to wood.
20 miles to water
6 inches to hell.
God bless our home.

The ones who stayed saw that the land quietly regained a measure of health. To their simple log cabins they added on rooms, resulting in what became a distinctly Texan style of architecture. Small towns sprung up where farmers and ranchers could trade their goods, places with friendly names like Hye, Blanco, Stonewall, Johnson City, and Albert.

As a consequence of the elements dealt them by the Hill Country, the people developed a strong strain of independence. Their region was the birthplace of an agrarian, populist political tradition that would forever see the small farmer as a greater good. Teetering precariously on the brink of disaster if they could not achieve self-sufficiency, they began to realize the tentativeness of their existence in this land.

From this somehow curious mixture of eastern and western values, in which the individual and the lessons of the past counted, rose a man who would move to the seat of power of the strongest nation of the world. But by the time Lyndon Baines Johnson ascended to the presidency of the United States, the world had changed immeasurably. Perhaps that fact, more than any other, made him yearn to hear the voice of his grandfather.

Cowboy camp near Round Mountain, circa 1900

Johnson Country

When Jesse Johnson died in May 1856 his estate was appraised at $2,740. He owed $2,331. The year following his death, a probate court gave his widow and his sons 125 bushels of corn "for their support and maintenance." Only a decade earlier Jesse Johnson had GTT, Gone to Texas, from Georgia, like many a hard-bitten southern farmer who had headed west in search of a better life.

Jesse was Lyndon Baines Johnson's great-grandfather. Jesse's tenth son, Sam Ealy Johnson Sr., was seventeen when his father died. Left to fend for themselves, Sam and his brother Tom proclaimed themselves stock raisers in Caldwell County, Texas.

By the time young Sam enlisted in the Confederate Army in 1861, he and Tom owned sixty horses and some cattle. Temporarily abandoning interest in the family business, he chose to defend his secessionist homeland. Tall, black-haired, twenty-two-year-old Sam joined a cavalry unit that was to serve "for the duration of the war."

The Caldwell County Rangers were a disciplined group of horse soldiers with strong esprit. Private Johnson's regiment made something of a name for itself with its spectator-pleasing drills and military ceremonies. Sam Johnson and the Rangers saw action at Galveston, and later received marching orders for Louisiana.

Near Mansfield the federal troops "were so near that the Caldwell County Rangers could hear their voices, the neighing of their horses, and the thud of their hooves. . . ." Fighting began and continued for two days. Young Private Johnson watched men get killed, and his own horse was shot out from under him. Through the humid Louisiana summer the handsome horse soldiers lost some of their polish and became malnourished and wracked by disease. Upon their return to Texas in May 1865, the restless troops were finally discharged.

Sam went home to find that half-wild Texas longhorn cattle had proliferated on the open range. With his brother Tom, he seized the opportunity to assemble a herd from the strays and ones bought on credit. With his new wife, Eliza Bunton, he moved to a dogtrot log cabin near the Pedernales River in the Hill Country.

Conditions were ripe for the industry to boom. Postwar cities in the North were hankering for beef, out-of-work soldiers were willing to learn how to handle a rope, and the railroads were vigorously making inroads into the western frontier. One essential ingredient was missing: a terminus point where the drovers, after trailing their herds more than a thousand miles, could sell their cattle and have them shipped to northern and eastern markets.

An ambitious Illinoisan of "advanced vision," Joseph Geiting McCoy, stepped in to fill the void. He struck a deal with the Union Pacific Railroad, snagged favorable freight rates, and settled on the dusty prairie town of Abilene, Kansas, as the site for shipping yards.

What McCoy found at Abilene was not much—a saloonkeeper who sold prairie dogs as tourist curiosities, his saloon, a six-room hotel, and a dry goods store. The energetic McCoy set to work and by the end of that summer the stockyards were finished and ready for customers.

Sam and Tom Johnson undoubtedly saw the circulars sent to Texas newspapers advertising the new facilities. McCoy boasted that the route to Abilene had "altogether better grass and fewer flies." They also were keenly aware that a cow that sold for four or five dollars in Texas would bring forty or fifty dollars in Abilene. In 1870 they drove 7,000 head of rangy longhorns to Kansas, returning with the tidy sum of $100,000 in gold. After they paid their debts, they bought more cattle on credit and in the summer of 1871 the brothers headed north with 10,000 head, sixteen cowboys to keep them in line, a cook and his chuck wagon loaded with plenty of bacon and beans, and a remuda of cow ponies.

Texas longhorn

Chisholm Trail

They followed the Chisholm Trail, a route that meandered through Austin and Fort Worth, across the Red River, through the Indian Nations in what is now Oklahoma, and across the border into Abilene.

The hardy, long-legged longhorn was made for the trail, "a traveling animal who incidentally carried beef on his bones," in the words of Texas historian Joe Frantz. But a disturbance, like lightning, a loud noise, or the smell of a wolf, could send them into a frenzy. A cowboy lullaby might prevent a stampede, or drovers might even sew shut the eyes of the ones they believed to be the instigators. Once a stampede occurred on a drive, though, a recurrence was not unusual.

When they started to wade the cattle across the Colorado River near Austin, the Johnson's herd stampeded. Cowboy A. W. Capt, who was along on the drive, reported frequent stampedes, plentiful dust, and "gyp water and poor chuck" as the bill of fare. On the return trip in November, the Johnsons followed another route back to Texas.

Young Horace Mark Hall, hired on for the trip home, wrote that a "Mrs. Johnson" rode ahead with him to scout. Whether this was Eliza is open to question. The historical record is incomplete. What we do know, though, is that Eliza was of hardy homesteader stock. Her father, Robert Bunton, had also trailed cattle to distant markets. Her uncle, of whom she often spoke, was John Wheeler Bunton, who signed the Texas Declaration of Independence, served on the front line at the battle of San Jacinto, and was a famed Indian fighter. He had pushed westward and built a plantation on the outer edges of the frontier, the frontier at that time being the Texas Hill Country.

Berry Roebuck (who drove cattle with Sam Sr.) shows LBJ and his daughter Lynda Bird where Eliza Bunton hid during the Indian raid.

For Eliza the alternative to making the rigorous ride up the Chisholm Trail was to stay at the cabin on the Pedernales through the scorching hot summer, tending her garden and trying not to dwell on thoughts of Comanche raiders who had killed a neighboring family. Shortly after the family was murdered, she was out drawing water from the spring when a cloud of dust on the horizon signaled a band of Indians riding toward the cabin. Legend has it that she grabbed her baby and crawled under the cabin, listening while the Indians ransacked the house and took horses from the barn. She waited until nightfall, when Sam returned, to come out of hiding.

The Johnson family, 1897. *Left to right:* LBJ's uncle, Thomas Jesse Johnson; aunt, Jessie Johnson; great grandmother, Priscilla Jane McIntosh Bunton; grandmother, Eliza Bunton Johnson; grandfather, Sam Johnson Sr.; aunt, Kate Johnson; aunt, Ava Johnson; aunt, Frank Johnson Martin; cousin, Thomas Johnson Martin; uncle, George Desha Johnson. The cabin later served as Lyndon's birthplace.

Eliza's patrician features, dark piercing eyes, porcelain skin, and imposing height are mentioned often by those who knew Lyndon B. Johnson's grandmother. While she always remembered what she called her "glorious" Bunton heritage, she was never free of the isolation and the plain hard work that were the lot of every pioneer woman. The log cabin was her civilization, and life hinged on her ability to save seeds from the previous summer's garden. She bore children and kept them well without benefit of a doctor or hospital, which meant maintaining a good supply of mustard plasters and flax seed poultices. Sanitation was a challenge. In the spring Eliza devoted days to making soap from the ashes and lye she saved. Since the ranch doubled as headquarters for the cattle operations, corrals were of necessity close to the house. Maddening flies were a plague to be endured.

Spinning wheel such as pioneer women used to make clothing

A fire was kept alive in the cabin's immense stone fireplace day and night. By banking a log at the back of the fireplace, burning coals would always be ready to ignite the breakfast fire. Eliza was up at daybreak to cook cornbread in the cast iron baker and parch green coffee beans in a skillet.

In the time left over after they secured and prepared food, pioneer women made clothing for their families. Wool and cotton were spun on the wooden spinning wheel and woven into linsey woolsey, a nearly indestructible fabric from which pants and shirts could be stitched. Brighter colors were obtained by dyeing the yarn with onion skins, mistletoe, or pecans. For Eliza a few yards of red and yellow calico for a dress would be a luxury. On a hot August afternoon Eliza might sneak a restful moment to sit in her rocker in the breezeway between the two rooms of the cabin.

The days at the settlement were coming to an end for Eliza and Sam, though. The 1871 trail drive had proved disastrous for the Johnson brothers. Supply of beeves began to exceed demand, forcing Tom and Sam to sell at rock bottom prices to make payments on their note. Sam and Eliza left Blanco County for the nearby plains to the east. It would be nearly fifteen years before they could return to the hills, and to do so Eliza sold one of the last remnants of her heritage, a handsome silver-mounted carriage that had been a wedding present. With the money, she and Sam bought another farm on the Pedernales in 1887, near what is now the small town of Stonewall.

They found life in the Hill Country changed. Settlers had flocked to Texas by the hundreds of thousands in the 1800s, preferring the "high healthy climate" of the hills to that of East Texas, "where even the alligators have chills and fevers," at least according to the *Blanco News*. These newcomers strung barbed wire around their homesteads, effectively closing off the range to free-roaming longhorns.

Historians now set 1885 as the year that spelled the end of the swashbuckling cowboy-cattle era of which Sam Johnson had been so much a part. Widespread use of wire fencing, combined with an extremely bad winter, dealt the death blow. Sam turned to raising cotton and corn on his new farm, with a brief foray into populist politics as a candidate for the People's Party. Eliza helped make ends meet for the family with the egg-and-butter money she kept sequestered in an old trunk.

For thirty more years they struggled. Sam Sr. and Eliza lived long enough to see their first son, Sam Ealy Jr., become established and firmly stamp the family name on the Pedernales Valley. It was, said the son, "Johnson Country."

Sam Ealy Johnson's cabin, restored at Lyndon Baines Johnson National Historical Park

LBJ speaking on the east porch of his boyhood home. Standing to his right is cousin Tom Martin, seated to his left Rebekah Baines Johnson and Lady Bird Johnson.

The Fledgling Years

Lyndon Johnson's parents could have saved themselves some trouble by simply naming their son Sam Ealy Johnson III. Instead, for the first several months of his life, Lyndon was called simply "baby." As the story goes, his father, Sam Ealy Jr., and his mother, Rebekah Baines, could not agree what to call their "bright and bonny" first child. Finally one morning Rebekah refused to prepare breakfast until they had named the boy. She disliked Sam's first two ideas, Clarence and Dayton. Then Sam suggested Linden, after a friend. Rebekah approved, but only if it could be spelled *Lyndon,* which she said was far more "euphonious." With the issue settled, she got up and made the biscuits.

Rebekah Baines Johnson

Sam Ealy Johnson Jr.

The night Lyndon was born the creeks in the Hill Country were on the rise. The doctor, twenty miles away, could not make it to the Johnson farm. Grandpa Sam hopped on his horse, Old Reb, and rode to fetch the midwife, Mrs. Lindig. At daybreak on August 27, 1908, Lyndon Baines Johnson was born, in the west room of the family's small house on the Pedernales River.

A year earlier Sam Ealy Jr. and Rebekah Baines had married. They met when Rebekah, a college-educated journalist, interviewed the "dashing and dynamic" state legislator. She found Sam "cagey" and hard to pin down with answers to her questions. But a courtship soon blossomed, most of which the couple spent attending political meetings and speeches.

The year Lyndon was born Sam Ealy Jr. decided not to run for a third term in the Texas legislature because his five-dollar-a-day salary wouldn't support a family. Instead he went back to farming and started to dabble in real estate. Farming was not really Sam's forte. He could cultivate cotton as a cash crop and sell it at the gin, but what he had always wanted to be was a teacher or lawyer. Poised and confident, with a quick mind and good memory, Sam had struggled to earn the education he knew he needed to attain his goal. When the chance came to run for the Eighty-Ninth District of the Texas House of Representatives, Sam jumped at it. He was twenty-seven years old, but he acted as no stranger to the cloakrooms in Austin, often voting with the minority for the populist ideals his father had preached. The *Gillespie County News* reported in 1905 that the "Hon. S. E. Johnson . . . accomplishes his ends by quiet and consistent attention to duty . . . and consistently refraining from the making of speeches."

His and Rebekah's first year on the farm by the Pedernales meant big adjustments for Rebekah. Her father, who had taught her "to study" and "to think," had been a lawyer and secretary of the state of Texas. Compared to the fine houses where her family had lived in Blanco and Fredericksburg, the farmhouse was solitary and rough. But her father had also taught her to endure; Rebekah soon acknowledged that her "strange new way of life" was "earnest and not the charming fairy tale" of her girlhood dreams.

Her baby boy, Lyndon, was her joy.

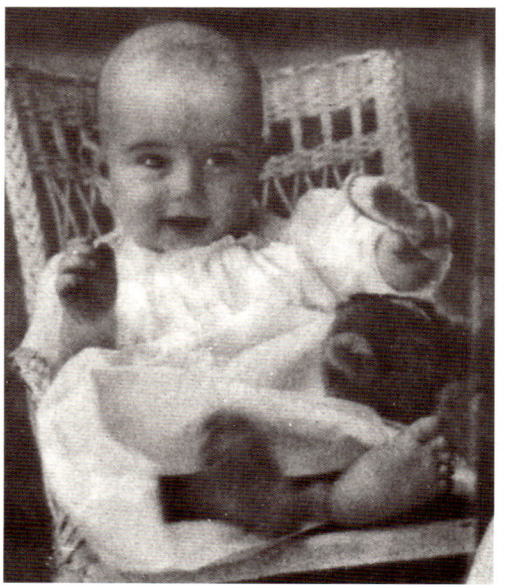

First picture of Lyndon at six months

Johnson City, Texas, circa 1900-1910

She worried constantly about him when he played by the river. At a young age he was an adventurous wanderer, causing Rebekah to install a dinner bell in the front yard that she could ring to summon help to search for her son. With his dog "Bigham Young," Lyndon would invariably head up the road to his grandparents' house, or up to the one-room Junction School where he could find his cousins.

At age three Lyndon received from Grandpa Sam a horse and saddle of his own. His cousin Ava, four years older, also got one. Recalled Ava, "Grandpa would say, 'Sit up in that saddle and throw your shoulders back.' We'd sit up and ride like little veterans." To Sam Sr. this was serious business. One of his favorite mottoes was "You can tell a man by his boots and his hat and the horse he rides."

By the time Lyndon was seven, Sam and Rebekah were convinced that farming was no way out of debt. In 1913 they moved to Johnson City, then a town of some three hundred souls, named for Sam Ealy Johnson Sr.'s nephew James Polk Johnson, who in 1879 platted it and secured its place as county seat. The move may have pleased Rebekah, for it provided her with an opportunity to write and teach. But Johnson City was still not Fredericksburg. The sight of a flock of turkeys being herded down Johnson City's Main Street, which was dust or mud depending on the weather, raised few eyebrows. A wooden sidewalk ran in front of a row of stores. There was one cafe, sometimes open for lunch, a bank, a school, several churches, and the courthouse. The most reliable transportation in or out was by horse-drawn vehicle.

Lyndon outside the boyhood home

The Johnsons bought one of the nicer homes in town, a three-bedroom white frame "gingerbread" house at the corner of 9th Street and Avenue G. Only later did they have a bathtub inside the house, with cold running water (hot water was obtained by heating kettlefuls on the wood stove). Sam's office was the enclosed breezeway where the hand-crank phone on the wall rang with all the town's party lines. The three girls, Rebekah, Josefa, and Lucia, had a room off one side of the office, while another door entered the dining room, the scene of lively dinnertime gabfests. Sam delighted in challenging his children to question-and-answer sessions, a debate, or a spelling bee. Many an evening was spent with all ears turned to a battery powered Atwater Kent table radio.

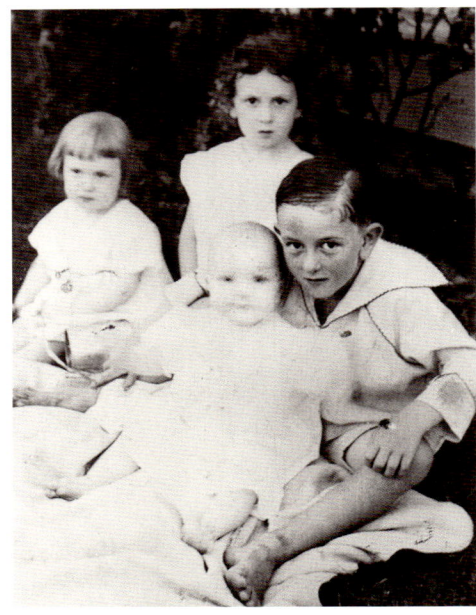

Lyndon holding his younger brother, Sam, with sisters, *left to right,* **Josefa and Rebekah**

The living room, or parlor, was the site of Rebekah's famous elocution lessons. Cousin Ava Johnson Cox remembers well the painful shyness and lack of confidence that had to be overcome to stand before Rebekah's mirror and recite. As she recalled, at least three young people would be in the parlor; "you were judged the minute you entered on how you carried yourself, how you sat down, and what you did. Hands had to be folded, shoulders back, chin in, and look straight ahead." Rebekah sat back in a corner with a pad taking notes on the students' expressions as they recited poetry, debated, or gave extemporaneous speeches.

Restored boyhood home

Lyndon's bedroom at the boyhood home

On the wall above the mantle in the living room hung a picture called "All is Vanity." At first glance it is a skull, staring back diabolically at the viewer. After a few minutes, and a closer look, a person might see the skull become a woman sitting before a dresser mirror. The picture, Rebekah said, taught that first impressions can be deceiving, that one should not make quick judgments.

Rebekah, with her cultured upbringing, wanted the same for her children. She tried to persuade Lyndon to play the violin, but he wasn't interested. He did, however, learn well from her the art of debate. For young Lyndon, his parents were the warp and weft of his life. From his mother he acquired the value of an education and from his father the pragmatic art of politics—the personal Texas style that would be his throughout his career.

After Sam Jr. reentered the legislature in 1918, Lyndon journeyed with him to Austin to attend legislative sessions, hurrying behind his father, listening to conversations, and soaking up meanings. President Johnson was to say, later, "I would sit in the gallery for hours watching all the activity on the floor and then wander around the halls trying to figure out what was going on." The only thing he loved more was going out into the hills, from one farm to another, talking with the farmers. He and his father would stop along the road when they were hungry and eat a slice of homemade bread with jam. Of his father Lyndon said, "I'd never seen him happier."

At night at home Lyndon would crouch by a bedroom window, straining to hear the soft voices of his father and his friends on the front porch of their Johnson City home.

The Fledgling Years

19

The Johnson children, *left to right:* Lucia, Josefa, Rebekah, Lyndon, and Sam

On one occasion, when the governor of Texas came to dinner on the Fourth of July, Lyndon huddled under the table to listen to the political talk. Often he would ignore his friends beckoning him to play, choosing instead to sit on the swing and discuss the burning issues of the day with his father.

Of course, Lyndon was still a boy, and at age twelve in a small Texas town, politics was not all there was to life. Lyndon's long reach earned him the nickname "FBJ," First Base Johnson, on the local sandlot baseball team. The Johnson City regulars would square off against Blanco or Stonewall and the rivalry was intense. No doubt young Lyndon traded his share of baseball cards like thousands of other boys in America during the 1920s. Energy and inventiveness overcame the lack of material goods. Barn lofts, rich with the scent of fresh hay, animals, and oiled leather, were ideal places for rough-housing, having corncob fights, or shooting rubber guns. Lyndon played a mean game of marbles, and from the veterans around the courthouse square he picked up the fine points of dominoes. The "Johnson Treatment" at the game was awesome to behold, according to Lyndon's brother Sam Houston, who saw him skunk many an opponent.

Lyndon "First Base" Johnson with friend Tom Crider at bat

Even as a youngster, Lyndon Johnson was an enterprising sort. At the "Lyndon Johnson Shoe Shine Shop" a man could get a spit shine for a nickel, which quickly found its way to Fawcett's Drugstore where it could be exchanged for a single-dip ice cream cone. Along with his schoolmates, Lyndon would trudge into the bare winter hills to run trap lines. Cotton was always there for the picking, and brought a dollar to

Lyndon with classmates at Johnson City High School, 1924

Johnson City, circa 1920

the one who could bag a hundred pounds in a day. Household chores—bringing in wood for the stoves, gathering eggs, or slopping hogs—were routine for Lyndon and his brother and sisters. At the age of twelve, he demonstrated the first signs of being a good administrator: Sam Houston, young Rebekah, Josefa, and Lucia were delegated specific tasks by their older brother, who appointed himself overseer of the work.

The Casparis's Cafe was the best (and only) lunch spot in Johnson City. Tall, lanky Lyndon would run in at noon and order a Texas T-bone. Fannie Casparis, without blinking an eye, would slide a big bowl of chili in front of him.

Parties, box suppers, and picnics were all part of the Johnson City social scene. On Friday or Saturday night Lyndon might have a date with a classmate, and they would go to a dance or to the Opera House above the bank to take in a Tom Mix western. On Sunday afternoons the family would pile into Sam's Model T, with its rubber horn and shiny brass lights and radiator, for a tour to a nearby town.

On May 4, 1924, Lyndon Johnson gave the commencement address at Johnson City High School. At fifteen, he was the youngest member of the class of six students, and though he encountered little trouble with his studies he announced, to his parents' chagrin, that he was done with school forever. Lyndon was a teenager with high ambitions and a strong case of wanderlust.

After traveling to California and returning home two years later "with empty hands and empty pockets," Lyndon took a sunup to sundown job on a road crew, driving a truck and a fresno. Before long, the nature of the job and his parents' persistence wore

With his savings of eighteen dollars, Lyndon joined five other young men, bought an old canvas-top car, and set out for California on a July day.

On the fifteen-hundred-mile trip they camped by

Left to right: cousin Tom Martin, Lyndon, and friends Fritz Koeniger and Otto Crider in California, 1925

railroad tracks, ate fatback, cornbread and molasses, and kept a close eye on their money. When they reached southern California, they found that fruit pickers and dishwashers were in demand. Though his fellow travelers finally turned back, Lyndon stayed in California for two more years, working as a law clerk for a relative in San Bernardino.

The Fledgling Years

Kleberg's Aide

nov. 1931

Lyndon B. Johnson Named Secretary To Richard M. Kleberg

Above is a likeness of Lyndon B. Johnson, '30, who, Monday's papers asserted, has been appointed private secretary to Richard M. Kleberg, congressman-elect from the fourteenth congressional district to succeed the late Harry M. Wurzbach. Lyndon is a well known figure on the Hill, having spent, off and on, several years here as student and part-time employee of the College, during which he was editor of the Star in the summer of '29 and secretary to President Evans during the session of 1929-30. Throughout his stay here he was a good student and very prominent in extra curricular activities, especially forensics and dramatics.

Lyndon, who is a native of Johnson City which in its turn was named for his grandfather, has had teaching experience at Cotulla and Houston. At the time of his appointment he was instructor in the department of speech in Sam Houston High School, Houston. The appointment carries with it an excellent salary as well as fine opportunities for social, cultural and political preferment. Lyndon's friends here are rejoicing in his good fortune, and wish him much success in his new position.

him down. Lyndon announced plans to go to college. A call to the college at San Marcos, fifty miles from Johnson City, had him enrolled for the new semester.

Given his background and his inclinations, Lyndon knew he would end up a teacher, a preacher, or a politician. Following in his father's footsteps, he earned a teaching certificate and taught in the small south Texas town of Cotulla and later in Houston. But the college president at San Marcos counseled him to enter public service where his competitive drive could be satisfied by meeting and handling immediate challenges that affected people's lives.

Every year since he was ten years old Lyndon had gone with his father to the July

Fourth picnic at the village of Henley. It was politics on the stump in the highest Texas fashion. When local candidate Pat Neff was called up front to the wagon platform to deliver his speech, he did not come forward. Lyndon, then a senior in college, stepped up and gave a speech in Neff's behalf. Welly Hopkins, a state senate candidate, quickly asked Lyndon to run his campaign. A year later U.S. Congressman Richard Kleberg offered Lyndon a job as his legislative secretary in his Washington, D.C., office. At four o'clock on a winter afternoon in 1931 Lyndon Johnson boarded the eastbound train for the city where he would live for thirty-seven years. Friends and relatives waved good-bye. "I tried to say something important to my mother," Lyndon recalled, "but I couldn't think of anything to say. When the train came, I felt relieved. I kissed my parents and climbed aboard."

On a trip to Austin in 1934 Lyndon Johnson met and two months later married Claudia Taylor. Known to him by her childhood nickname, Lady Bird, she stayed with him throughout his years in the nation's

LBJ and Lady Bird on their honeymoon in Mexico, November 1934

capital and during his retirement at their ranch in the Hill Country. He proved himself a hard worker as secretary to Congressman Kleberg, and in 1935 he was named to head President Franklin D. Roosevelt's National Youth Administration in Texas. His 1937 campaign for the U.S. Congress was successful, and he represented his constituents in the Tenth District for twelve years before Texans elected him to the Senate. His political star rising, Lyndon Johnson became majority leader of the Senate. The assassination of John F. Kennedy in 1963 brought Vice-President Johnson to the presidency of the United States.

The Johnson family in 1934. *Left to right:* Sam Jr., Lyndon, Rebekah Baines, Sam Houston, Rebekah Luruth, Josefa, unidentified, Lucia, unidentified

The Fledgling Years

Nellie Connally, LBJ, and Lady Bird look on as Texas Governor John Connally speaks at a 1967 presidential party on the banks of the Pedernales.

Heart's Home

WHERE ELSE BUT IN THE HILL COUNTRY OF TEXAS WOULD THE HEAD OF THE GERMAN GOVERNMENT BE HOSTED AT A STATE DINNER IN A HIGH SCHOOL gymnasium, complete with authentic barbecue, a rendition of "Deep in the Heart of Texas" sung in German, and a classical piano concert by Van Cliburn? President Lyndon B. Johnson staged just such a gala in Stonewall down the road from his ranch for German Chancellor Ludwig Erhard, and the gym was packed to the rafters. His was a presidential style that was, to say the least, novel to the Washington press corps, Secret Service entourage, cabinet members, and anyone else accustomed to following a president of the United States. His style and character remained grounded in the Texas Hill Country where, as his father had told him, "people knew when you were sick and cared when you died."

Ranch Road One, just off Highway 290 on the south side of the Pedernales River, passes in front of the Lyndon B. Johnson ranch, also known as the Texas White House. In 1951 then-Senator Johnson bought the rambling white house and land from his Aunt Frank. Lyndon had long admired the place and had spent many hours there visiting his aunt and uncle. It was part of the valley that was "Johnson Country." Mrs. Johnson knew that a big job lay ahead of them to make the place their home.

The Texas White House prior to renovation

One "Polecat" Meier, a German immigrant from nearby Fredericksburg, had built the original portion of the house. The Meiers started with a simple one-room cabin with loft, and for a time cooked their meals over an open fire behind the cabin. Around 1894 the Rock House, now the west wing of the existing ranch house, was built by three German stonemasons using hand hewn native limestone from nearby Gillespie County hills.

For another twelve years the Meier family lived in this two-story frame "ell." Finally, after the property had changed hands several more times, Lyndon Johnson's Aunt Frank and Uncle Clarence Martin bought it.

Soon after the Johnsons purchased the ranch, Senator Johnson tackled his first priority—a dam and low-water crossing on the Pedernales River that would create a reservoir for irrigation and give better access to the main road. At the same time, Mrs. Johnson's primary concern was the live oak trees in the front yard, so an Austin tree surgeon was hired to prune and care for them. Throughout the fifties and sixties the Johnsons continued to improve and add to the house and grounds—bedrooms, office, airstrip, and swimming pool. Though they lived in Washington, D.C., the ranch came to be, in Mrs. Johnson's words, their "heart's home."

On the doormat at the front door to the house are the words "All The World Is Welcome Here." Texas hospitality flowed freely at the ranch. On Christmas in 1963, just after Lyndon Johnson had become president, he escorted the press around the grounds. They surveyed the airplane hangar, the livestock pens, and the dam, then received a tour inside the comfortably furnished house. The president's attire, khakis, boots, and a cowboy hat, bore little resemblance to his usual city dress, but suited him far better.

LBJ with Aunt Frank

It was on this same trip that the festivities were held in honor of Chancellor Erhard. One reporter, Frank Cormier, found the menu, for a state dinner, "unique." The crowd downed "four hundred pounds of beef, three hundred pounds of ribs, more than one hundred pounds of German potato salad, one hundred pounds of coleslaw, twenty-five gallons of ranch

The Texas White House after remodeling

beans, seventy gallons of beer and ample amounts of coffee and soft drinks." To top it all off, the president handed out Texas hats "to every German in sight."

A nearly constant round of parties, informal press conferences, rides in the president's white Lincoln (fully equipped with bullhorn), and visits to neighboring farms and ranches kept the press men and women on their toes. Though the ranch may have been President Johnson's refuge from the pressures of his job, many around him found the pace less than restful. Mrs. Johnson would graciously make room on a moment's notice for yet one more unexpected guest, the cook had to make sure food was waiting in the kitchen for the president's midnight snacks, and ranch hands answered unending questions as they tried to load cattle into a chute. The president routinely watched three television sets at once, and a telephone was always by his side, even in the pool. One entire building housed a communications system that could provide instantaneous international connections.

LBJ and members of the international press converse on Texas White House lawn, 1967

LBJ entertains dinner guests, July 1968

On Sundays after church President Johnson would extend an invitation: "I'm going to see some pretty country . . . You-all can come along if you want to." And as Cormier recalled, twenty or thirty cars would join the parade, bumping over dusty roads to go pass the time of day with a neighbor. A favorite excursion was a twilight stroll up the road to Cousin Oreole Bailey's house. A half dozen reporters would trail along to her modest house, whose walls bore a color portrait of Lyndon and one of his campaign posters. She and the president would exchange banterings and, warned the president, one had to be "mentally awake" when visiting Cousin Oreole.

Lyndon's earliest memories were of this land—walking across dry fields, through hot sand along the banks of the Pedernales. In a speech given in 1965 President Johnson gave a crystal clear recollection: "Those hills and those fields and that river were the only real world that I really had in those years. So I did not know much about how much more

The reconstructed birthplace

Not far from Mrs. Bailey's house was Lyndon Johnson's birthplace, a site that would capture more of his and Mrs. Johnson's attention as the years passed. The birthplace was reconstructed by Austin architect J. Roy White, who was able to locate old rock foundations and indications of a house of several rooms. With the help of relatives, he obtained enough information to draw a floor plan. He concluded that it had been a typical Texas farmhouse with an open central hallway, or dogtrot, between two large rooms. The house had a porch, a kitchen at the back, and an underground cistern. By August 1964, reconstruction of the birthplace was complete. Before tour operations were turned over to the National Park Service in 1969, local women guided visitors through it, pointing out the west room where Lyndon was born on that rainy night.

beautiful it was than that of many other boys, for I could imagine nothing else from sky to sky. Yet the sight and the feel of that country somehow or other burned itself into my mind."

When he wasn't entertaining international dignitaries or talking to reporters, the president closely supervised his ranch. At the heart of the operation was a herd of Hereford cattle, registered and commercial. A far cry from the Texas longhorn, the genteel Hereford hails from England. Handsome animals, with their white face and markings on reddish-brown bodies, they dot the hillsides like so many porcelain figurines. They also make good hamburgers and steaks.

The Johnson herd was built from ten registered Herefords that the president bought in 1957. Bulls, primarily from the Husker-Mischief bloodline, were bred with heifers in the spring and fall. Care of the calves has changed little: As soon as a calf is born the ears are tagged, and for the registered animals pedigree information is recorded for future sale. At three months they are vaccinated, and at seven months they are weaned and weighed. At this age these "baby" cows already tip the scales at close to a marketable six hundred pounds.

To keep them healthy and growing, the president's cattle were fed a ration of half crimped oats, another third or so of milo or corn, and cotton hull and protein supplement. In summer two cows and calves could be run on an acre of the ranch's irrigated Bermuda grass.

Occasionally the registered Herefords from the Johnson ranch would be shown at local fairs and livestock shows. In the show barn on the hill these animals were "fitted"—groomed, trained, and readied for exhibition. A show animal faced exacting criteria. It needed to possess a straight back, good body pattern with a clean middle, trim belly and brisket, wide loin, thick rear end, and straight legs. The animal's horns were weighted on each end so that they would turn down and frame the face. Its hair was washed, combed, curled, and blown dry in preparation for showing.

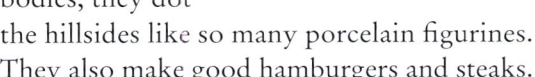
LBJ examines a little heifer, 1968

Hereford body types are rated on a scale from one to seven, based on the height of the hip from the ground. The best cattle on the Johnson ranch in the late sixties and early seventies approached a type five, a taller, longer animal than had been in demand previously. Consumer preference at the time dictated meat with less fat, and cattle breeders acquiesced.

The president stopped showing cattle from the ranch around 1966. Instead, while Herefords were still bred and sold, President Johnson aimed the ranch at self-sufficiency.

Lyndon working one of his prized registered Herefords, circa 1963

On nearby land Angora goats were raised for mohair, and Rambouillet and Columbia sheep were sheared for wool and sold as Easter lambs. Pigs and chickens were part of the program too. Peppery sausage, made straight from a ranch porker, was a favorite in the Texas White House. At one point two to three hundred laying hens were giving eggs that found their way into specially designed red-white-and-blue cartons. A garden of nearly two acres was planted with all manner of vegetables—corn, black-eyed peas, green beans, okra, potatoes, and onions. He sold eggs and butter locally, and he was known to load three hundred pounds of potatoes on the plane to take back to Washington. Lyndon Johnson may have been the only president in recent history to furnish the Washington White House table with produce from his own garden.

Few details of work on the ranch escaped his notice. Whether it was laying irrigation pipe, making sure water troughs were clean, or inquiring about a particular heifer's condition, he was fully versed in the

September 1967

operations. When President Johnson retired from public life and returned to the ranch, he ran it like it was the federal government, calling staff meetings of all hands each morning and barking orders over the phone to a parts supplier.

On a warm day in January 1969 former President Lyndon Johnson, with Mrs. Johnson, returned for good to the Texas Hill Country. Ranch foreman Dale Malechek

The president's funeral, January 1973

and his wife Jewell, along with the Catholic priest, Lutheran minister, and local ranchers and townspeople, were there to greet them. "They all looked as if they were glad to see us, and God knows we were glad to see them," said the president.

He was still their favorite son, and many of them had known him all his life. Some had known his father and grandfather too. Perhaps better than people in the nation's capital, they understood his earthiness and the basis for his belief that anything was possible if a man worked hard enough. Certainly they were the direct beneficiaries of many of Lyndon Johnson's values—the overriding importance of an education (he had signed a landmark federal education law at the Junction School) and the need for rural electrification (through his efforts one of the world's largest rural electrical cooperatives is headquartered in Johnson City). Too, they were no strangers to his personal intense style of politicking. He simply was emulating his father and many other Texas politicians before him. They laughed at his stories because they embodied characters who easily could have been their next-door neighbors.

Not long after he returned to his beloved Hill Country, Lyndon Johnson began to write his memoirs. He reminisced about his childhood, of his parents and especially his grandfather, sitting in his rocker, telling his eager young grandsons stories of tough cowboys and Civil War heroes. In an attempt to understand the complexities of his personality, one of his biographers insightfully wrote that he was a "child of the passing frontier. . . . His Americanism was the reflection of an America that is no longer ours."

On January 22, 1973, Lyndon Johnson suffered a heart attack. Mrs. Johnson was not home and before the Secret Service men arrived he had passed away, in his room alone at age sixty-four. Journalist Bill Porterfield described the day on which the president was buried alongside his parents and grandparents: In the freezing rain the live oaks "hung like mourners" over the tombstones in the family cemetery beside the Pedernales. Thousands of people "stood in puddles for hours awaiting his last trip home." Eulogies were given and a twenty-one-gun salute was delivered. His daughter Luci remembered a ninety-two-year-old black man at the graveside who she tried to comfort. He said, "Ma'am, you don't have to tell me he loved me. He showed he loved me. A tree would have had to fall over me to keep me from being here today."

Lyndon Johnson's father had been right. They cared when he died.

At the ranch, 1971

BIBLIOGRAPHY

Bearss, Edwin C. *Historic Resource Study: Lyndon B. Johnson National Historic Site.* Washington D.C.: U.S Department of Interior, National Park Service, 1971.

Bedichek, Roy. *Adventures with a Texas Naturalist.* Revised edition. Austin: University of Texas Press, 1966.

Bode, Elroy. *This Favored Place: The Texas Hill Country.* Bryan, Texas: Shearer Publishing, 1983.

Bones, Jim Jr. *Texas Heartland: A Hill Country Year.* Text by John Graves. College Station: Texas A&M Press, 1975.

Caro, Robert A. *The Path to Power: The Years of Lyndon Johnson,* Vol. 1. New York: Alfred A. Knopf, 1982.

Cormier, Frank. *LBJ: The Way He Was.* New York: Doubleday, 1977.

Dobie, J. Frank. *The Longhorns.* New York: Bramhall House, 1941.

Fehrenbach, T. R. *Lone Star: A History of Texas and the Texans.* New York: Macmillan, 1968.

Frantz, Joe B. *Texas: A Bicentennial History.* New York: W. W. Norton, 1976.

Gard, Wayne. *The Chisholm Trail.* Norman: The University of Oklahoma Press, 1954.

Gard, Wayne. *Rawhide Texas.* Norman, University of Oklahoma Press, 1965.

Graves, John. *Hard Scrabble: Observations on a Patch of Land.* New York: Alfred A. Knopf, 1974.

—— *Growing Up in Texas: Recollections of a Childhood.* Austin: Encino Press, 1972.

Johnson, Sam Houston. *My Brother Lyndon.* New York: Cowles Book Company, 1969.

Kearns, Doris. *Lyndon Johnson and the American Dream.* New York: Harper & Row, 1976.

Maguire, Jack, ed. *A President's Country: A Guide to the LBJ Country of Texas.* Austin: Shoal Creek Publishers, 1964.

Miller, Merle. *Lyndon: An Oral Biography.* New York: Ballantine Books, 1980.

Miller, Ray. *Eyes of a Texan Travel Guide.* Houston: Cordovan Corporation, 1980.

Olmstead, Frederick Law. *A Journey through Texas.* Reprint of 1857 edition. Austin: University of Texas Press, 1978.

Porterfield, Bill. *A Loose Herd of Texans.* College Station: Texas A&M Press, 1978.

Provence, Harry. *Lyndon B. Johnson: A Biography.* New York: Fleet Publishing Corporation, 1964.

Sidey, Hugh. *A Very Personal Presidency: Lyndon Johnson in the White House.* New York: Atheneum, 1968.

Steinberg, Alfred. *Sam Johnson's Boy: A Close-up of the President from Texas.* New York: Macmillan, 1968.

Webb, Walter Prescott. *The Great Plains.* Boston: Houghton Mifflin, 1931.